P9-CQB-194

WILLIAM VAN HORNE

CHRISTOPHER MOORE

CANADIAN PATHFINDERS SERIES

Cover illustration and pages 7, 13: Colin Gillies

Photo Credits: Public Archives of Canada, pages 9 (C8549), 23 (C14114), 30-31 (C3693), 36 (C63478); Metro Toronto Library Board, pages 14, 39; Canadian Pacific Corporate Archives, pages 16, 17, 18, 19, 20, 28, 29, 34, 35, 37, 38, 40; Glenbow Archives, pages 21, 42; Provincial Archives of British Columbia, page 27; Ontario Archives, page 33; Saskatchewan Archives, page 43; Provincial Archives of Alberta, page 44; Vancouver City Archives, page 45.

Canadian Cataloguing in Publication Data

Moore, Christopher
William Van Horne

(Canadian pathfinders series)
For use in schools.
Includes index.
ISBN 0-7172-2161-X

1. Van Horne, William Cornelius, Sir, 1843–1915. 2. Canadian Pacific Railway—Biography. I. Title. II. Series.

HE2808.2.V3M6 1987 j385'.065'710924 C87-093361-2

123456789 DWF 6543210987

Printed and Bound in Canada.

Contents

How To Be a Railway General

Over a hundred years ago, when William Cornelius Van Horne was young, railways were the most exciting invention around.

They were still very new then. The first railway had not been built until 1830, but after that they spread rapidly. The Industrial Revolution was on. There were new inventions, and new ways of working. Machines began to do jobs that had always been done slowly by hand, and they began to do other jobs that had never been possible before. The way ordinary people lived and worked began to change. Some people thought that everyone would live better because of machines.

The most impressive of all the new machines was the railway. In the horse-and-buggy era, before there were cars or telephones or electric lights, there was nothing like a great steam locomotive roaring down the tracks with a line of boxcars behind it. Railways were the biggest, noisiest, shiniest and most powerful machines around.

People who worked with railways felt important, and the most important of all were the people who built new railways.

Building a new railway was a big job. The builders needed lots of money, and they usually spent it as fast as it came in. They needed iron and steel and wood and explosives. They needed to hire hundreds or thousands of workers. There would be surveyors to plan the route, engineers to design the railway, and workers to clear the ground, lay the ties and hammer down the spikes. Somehow the planners, the workers, the tools, supplies and the money all had to be brought together in the right place at the right time.

They said in those days that anyone with a railway to build really needed a "railway general"—someone who could run the job the way a general runs an army. A railway general could do just about anything on a railway. He could tell the surveyors how to plan the route, tell the workers how to lay the track, and tell the managers how to write the train schedules. He could drive trains and plan stations and even write advertisements for his railway. People said that a real railway general could do all that twice as fast as anyone expected and spend half as much money.

In 1881 the Canadian Pacific Railway was the greatest railway-building project in the world. Canada had promised itself a rail line stretching from Montreal and the Atlantic coast all the way to the Pacific Ocean. It would have to cross mountain ranges, muskeg swamps and plains that belonged to the buffalo herds and the Indian nations. The man who took charge of building the Canadian Pacific Railway was William Van Horne. They called him the ablest railway general in the world.

The Boy Who Loved Railways

Running railways was always William Van Horne's dream. He was born in 1843 in the American state of Illinois. The United States was still expanding its territory then, and Illinois was part of its western frontier. Railways were helping to open the West, and it was easy for young William Van Horne to be impressed by them.

William's father was a country lawyer, but the family was often short of money. William, the oldest of five children, was a tough boy who got into a lot of fights. He could draw very well, he was interested in science and nature, and he worked hard when he wanted to. Once he hand-copied a whole book, pictures and all, just so he could have his own copy. When William was only eleven, his father died. Like many youngsters then, he knew he would soon have to leave school and go to work.

William got his first railway job in 1857. He was just fourteen when he began training to be a telegraph operator for the Illinois Central Railway. He liked the work. He thought railways were truly exciting, and every day he heard all the business of the line on his telegraph. Then one day, the Super came to town.

The Super—the General Superintendent of the railway—was the most important man young William Van Horne had ever seen. He rolled into town in his own special train, and he climbed down from his own private train car to inspect the station where Van Horne worked. As the Super walked through the buildings and yards giving instructions and organizing the whole railway, he seemed full of dignity and importance. Van Horne, who already loved railways, was greatly impressed by this man

Young William Van Horne enjoyed his job as a telegraph operator and worked hard at it. He worked even harder at taking advantage of the opportunities it gave him to learn everything there was to know about railways and how they operated.

who ran one. He made up his mind then and there. That was what he wanted: the power, the wealth and the private railway car. He was eighteen, and he decided he would be a railway Super in ten years.

"I imagined that a General Superintendent must know everything about a railway—every detail in every department," said Van Horne, so he began learning. He already knew the telegraph office, so he worked in the freight yard, at the ticket counter, in the repair shops and aboard the locomotives. He learned the complicated job of making up schedules for all the trains on his company's tracks. The American railway system was growing rapidly, and as Van Horne mastered different tasks, he moved into more important positions. He was becoming an important railway man.

It took Van Horne eleven years instead of ten to achieve his ambition, but he was still only twenty-nine when a new railway made him its General Superintendent in 1872. He was the youngest Super in the railway business.

All through the 1870s, he did what he liked best: building and running several railways in the western United States. Some of them were actually not very successful railways. One was laughingly described as "two streaks of rust along a right-of-way." Some were owned by dishonest men who wanted to be paid for railways they would never complete. However, Van Horne tried to build railways and run them well. Gradually, he received more and more authority over the railways and their workers.

Railway companies were harsh employers. They needed many workers, and they expected them to work hard. The work was often dangerous and there were few safety precautions. The workers had no unions, and those who complained or made demands could be fired. If the workers tried to

No matter how hard he worked at building and running railways, Van Horne somehow always had enough energy left over to pursue a wide range of hobbies. He was an avid reader, a keen collector of fossils and an enthusiastic gardener. Later in life, he developed a great passion for art and art collecting. He became an accomplished painter himself, and over the years, he acquired a magnificent collection of paintings and other objets d'art.

organize strikes, their organizations would be broken up, often with violence.

Van Horne knew all of this, for he had started near the bottom. To work his way to the top, he had to be as tough as every other railway Superintendent. Van Horne thought he was a fair boss, but he was tough. He demanded hard work and obedience, and he broke strikes and fired anyone who resisted his plans. That was part of being a railway general, too.

Word spread that William Van Horne was a real railwayman, someone who knew how to build railways and how to run them. By 1881 this reputation had spread to Canada, and from Canada came a great opportunity. With the biggest railway project in the world under way, Canada needed Van Horne to finish the job.

General Boss of Everybody and Everything

Until 1881 William Van Horne had never been to Canada, but railways were important here too. Hundreds of kilometres of railways had been built in Ontario and Quebec, and in 1876 a line had been completed all the way east to Halifax, Nova Scotia.

As the railways grew, Canada's cities and towns grew with them. Factories were built. Farmers used the railway to send their crops and livestock to towns far away, and merchants like Mr. Eaton of Toronto found they could sell their goods everywhere the railways went. Unlike the boats on rivers and canals that froze every winter, trains could run all year. They travelled faster and could carry much more freight than horse-drawn wagons could. There was a railway "mania" in Canada. Every town wanted a rail line of its own.

Railways could also help bind the new nation together. Canada had become a nation in 1867, when four provinces had joined together in Confederation. There were two provinces on the Atlantic coast—New Brunswick and Nova Scotia—and two further inland—Quebec and Ontario. A powerful persuader for the Maritime provinces to join Confederation was the Intercolonial Railway project. This railway would link the Atlantic provinces and Quebec. A few years later, when it was time to add the prairies and British Columbia to Confederation, a much greater railway project was born. Prime Minister John A. Macdonald announced that a railway must be built all the way to British Columbia and the Pacific Ocean. The new line would run through Canadian territory all the way, and it would be built in ten years.

When William Van Horne came to Canada in 1881, those ten years had passed, but the railway had barely been begun. It seemed impossible for a small new country with only three and a half million people to build a railway 4600 kilometres long. It would have to run through a wilderness of rock, swamp, plains and mountains that was populated mostly by Indian nations. The company that had been formed to build the railway had collapsed. Prime Minister Macdonald had resigned. And the new prime minister, Alexander Mackenzie, called the railway "an act of insane recklessness."

Still, a start had been made. Land treaties had been signed with the chiefs of the Indian nations. Surveyors and explorers had begun to search for the best route across the country, and railway crews had begun laying track around Winnipeg. By 1881 Sir John A. Macdonald was prime minister again and a new company had been formed to build the railway—the Canadian Pacific Railway Company, or CPR. But the work was going slowly, and the people in charge of construction seemed to be getting rich without getting their work done.

The CPR realized that it needed one person who could take charge of the whole huge operation. They hired William Van Horne, and he arrived in Winnipeg on the very last day of 1881.

When he took charge of the CPR, Van Horne was thirty-eight years old. He was married and had a son and a daughter. He was a big, tough, hardworking man with a beard, who usually had a cigar in his mouth. He loved to eat. He collected fossils and he grew roses. Sometimes he played the violin and sometimes he played poker. He was curious about nearly everything.

Railways had already made him rich, but he was still ambitious. Van Horne thought nothing was

Van Horne always looked forward to the time he could spend at home. Lucy Van Horne and the children, Adaline and Richard Benedict, received much adoring attention from Van Horne, who was as devoted and loving in his private life as he was demanding and hardworking in his public life.

impossible, and he loved the challenge of his new job. As he told a friend, he was not just a General Superintendent now. He was "general boss of everybody and everything" in the greatest railway project in the world.

William Van Horne had no doubt that he could get the job done.

Lucy Van Horne

Lucy Adaline Hurd was born in Galesburg, Illinois. She was educated at Lombard College in Galesburg and was described as tall, slender and dignified with black hair, hazel eyes and a lovely complexion. Because of her beauty and distinction, she was chosen to read the city's welcome address to Abraham Lincoln when he visited Galesburg in 1858.

Soon afterwards, she and her widowed mother moved to Joliet, Illinois, and she commuted weekly between Joliet and Chicago where she studied at Dr. Ziegfield's College of Music. It was on a trip home from Chicago that she chanced to meet William Van Horne at the Joliet train station. This was in 1864. Two years later Lucy Adaline and William Van Horne became engaged, and they married in March 1867.

The Van Hornes had three children—a daughter, Adaline, and two sons, William, who died at age five, and Richard Benedict. Lucy and William Van Horne were very devoted companions throughout their marriage. Together they established a warm, loving home environment, which they eagerly shared with family and close friends.

Eight Hundred Kilometres

Almost as soon as he arrived, Van Horne announced his plans for 1882. He declared that the Canadian Pacific Railway Company would lay 800 kilometres of track that year.

No one believed him. The railway had been under way for ten years, but it had less than 500 kilometres of track. In 1881 the company had used up all the supplies and equipment it had, just to build 150 kilometres of track.

In Winnipeg, Van Horne made his plans. Canada had no factories to make steel, so he ordered rails from England and Germany. Soon his old American railways were carrying them north to Winnipeg. From the lumber camps of Ontario came loads of roughly cut railway ties, and the storage yards began to fill with stone for the track bed. Contractors began to hire hundreds and then thousands of workers who were to build Van Horne's 800 kilometres of railway.

They gathered in Winnipeg that spring. There were young men from Ontario, Quebec and Nova Scotia. Up from the United States came hundreds of workers. Immigrants from Ireland and Italy and Sweden signed on. Native peoples explored the route and helped to build it. There were blacks in the work crews, and in British Columbia many of the workers were labourers from China. Some of the workers had been building railways for years. Others had never done hard work in their lives. Van Horne wanted trained workers, but he needed ten thousand of them, so he would hire almost anyone. At least, he would hire any man. In those days, railwaymen did not believe that women could build

The Navvy

"Navvy" was the name given to workers who built navigational canals. When these workers began to build railways instead, they took the name with them.

It was the navvies who built the Canadian Pacific Railway, and most of their work was done by hand. They did have dynamite to help them, and toward the end of the project, Van Horne brought in new track-laying machines to speed up the work. Most of the railway, however, was built with picks, shovels, wheelbarrows and horsedrawn ploughs.

Navvies were quite well paid, because railway building was an important job, but their pay ended as soon as the job was done, and the work was hard and dangerous. In the work camps, the men lived aboard trains or in bunkhouses. They ate stew and bread, they played cards, and they drank a lot, even though Van Horne tried to keep alcohol out of the camps.

No one knows for certain how many navvies worked on the CPR, or many of their names, or where they went afterwards. Some went back to Europe or China or the United States. Some became settlers in Canada, and some just went on to the next railway job. Before they left, a few of the navvies got together for their own last spike ceremony.

railways, and Van Horne's work crews did not hire any.

Track-laying started in April 1882, west of Winnipeg, Manitoba. At first things went slowly. By the end of May only sixty kilometres of track had been laid. It looked as if Van Horne would not be able to build the railway much faster than anyone else had.

Then construction started to roll. In June, the track began to move across the prairie at a speed no one had seen before. The centre of the action was a place called "End of Track."

Bunkhouses like these were home to many workers on the CPR. These accommodations provided the barest essentials and were a far cry from the luxurious accommodations Van Horne would insist upon for his passenger trains.

"End of Track was something more than just the point to which track had been laid," said one man who was there. "It was a real live community." There were wagon drivers, track-layers, blacksmiths, cooks, foremen and engineers at End of Track, and they all lived aboard a train that was like a town on wheels. The train had bunkhouses, dining halls and offices. As the workers laid track, their town on wheels and the supplies it carried moved with them. At the end of a day's work, End of Track could be five kilometres from where it had started in the morning.

MEN WANTED!

A number of Men will be wanted by the undersigned during the grading season this year on west end of CANADIAN PACIFIC RAILWAY. Wages will be

$1.50 PER DAY,

BOARD $4.50 PER WEEK,

During the Summer Months for good, able-bodied, steady men.

Apply on the work at end of track, now near Cypress Hills, about 600 miles west of Winnipeg.

LANGDON, SHEPARD & CO.,
CONTRACTORS.

END OF TRACK,
April 20th 1883

It took a lot of work to move End of Track that far. Out in front, survey crews marked the route, and horse-drawn ploughs and graders cleared a path twenty metres wide. Behind them, workers piled up a road-bed of rock and earth. Bridges were quickly built over every gully and creek. Then came the track-laying crews. One crew laid out thick wooden ties, and another hauled up the heavy steel rails, ten metres long and weighing 250 kilograms each. As the rail crew heaved the rails across the ties and set them in two precise lines, four spikes nailed the rails to each tie. Even before the spikes were hammered down, the tie-laying crews and the rail crews were moving ahead. Other crews came behind, building fences and telegraph lines and stations along the track. As the workers moved along, cooks and trainmen and managers worked aboard the trains. The noise of men, horses, hammers and steam engines hardly ever stopped.

Track could easily be set down at a rate of nearly four kilometres a day across the prairies, but the going was much slower in the mountains of British Columbia or along the northern shore of Lake Superior.

"Van Horne," wrote the Winnipeg Sun *in 1892, "is calm and harmless-looking. So is a she-mule, and so is a buzz-saw . . . . To see Van Horne get out of the car and go softly up the platform you would think he was an evangelist on his way west to preach temperance to the Mounted Police. But you are soon undeceived. If you are within hearing distance, you will have more fun than you ever had in your life before."*

The moving town called End of Track went a long way in 1882. It started in Manitoba and rolled slowly into Saskatchewan. Regina, the town that would one day be the capital of the province of Saskatchewan, was born that summer when End of Track passed through. When work stopped in the winter, End of Track had almost reached Alberta.

Van Horne's ten thousand men had built over 600 kilometres on the main line and 250 kilometres of side lines—more than 800 kilometres in one season. They had laid one and a half million ties, more than one for every metre of track. They had nailed 52 000 tonnes of rails to those ties, built thirty-two stations, and strung 1400 kilometres of

Crowfoot

Chief Crowfoot was about a dozen years older than Van Horne. While Van Horne was learning about railways in the United States, Crowfoot was leading his people, the Blackfoot nation of southern Alberta, in great buffalo hunts.

By the 1870s the buffalo, which had always provided the Plains Indians with all the necessities of life, were disappearing. Realizing that his people faced starvation, Crowfoot made a treaty with the government of Canada. He took his people to a reserve near Calgary, where he hoped they could become farmers.

Crowfoot hoped that new immigrants and settlers would obey the treaty and live at peace with his people, and he allowed the railway to be built across his reserve in 1883. In 1885 the Blackfoot were hungry and bitter, but Crowfoot persuaded them not to join the Northwest Rebellion. He knew that war would make things even worse for his people.

Van Horne admired Crowfoot. He thanked the Blackfoot chief for keeping the peace and gave him a lifetime pass for travel on the CPR. But Crowfoot knew when Van Horne's railway and all the other changes came to the prairies, that his way of life had ended. His last years were unhappy, for his people were still poor and hungry.

telegraph line. The CPR was going somewhere now!

The workers had learned that Van Horne was a tough boss who would do what he promised. That summer he was always on the move. When he suddenly arrived at End of Track in his private car, the workers would say he was "hot enough to melt the tracks" as he rushed around asking questions and demanding explanations. Van Horne wanted to know everything, and nothing could be done fast enough to suit him that summer.

Once he had asked all his questions, Van Horne would settle down. Since he loved to eat, he made sure that his workers had all the food and coffee they needed. In the evening, he might organize foot races or target shooting, or he might sit up all night playing poker. In the morning, he would jump up with his winnings and head back to Winnipeg, as if he needed no sleep. "I eat all I can, I drink all I can, I smoke all I can," he said. "What do you want to go to bed for? It's a waste of time!" Van Horne hated to waste time.

"Nothing is impossible," he loved to say. When one of his engineers told him they would have to stop for a year while one difficult tunnel was being built, Van Horne ordered him to take out the tunnel. "Fix it up!" he cried.

"Mr. Van Horne," said the engineer, "the mountains are in the way, and the rivers don't run in the right direction. Shall we fix them up too?"

Van Horne laughed out loud. That was the kind of attitude he liked. The engineer did find another route, and the railway went ahead.

Lakes, Rocks and Muskegs

In 1883, End of Track continued to move across the prairies. By the end of the year it had crossed Alberta and reached the slopes of the Rocky Mountains. But not everything had gone smoothly. When the CPR laid track across Indian reserves, the Indian peoples grew alarmed and angry. They had made treaties for their prairie lands, and they threatened war to defend them. Before the railway could proceed, the CPR had to persuade the Indian leaders to accept other lands for their reserves.

Meanwhile, William Van Horne had gone east to Ontario, for the railway also had to get through the wild land north of Lake Superior. This was not prairie. It was rocks, trees and lakes, and many experts had said it would be impossible to build a railway there. Fifteen thousand men worked on that part of the CPR, and they found it was difficult, dangerous work.

Dougherty's Cut. Building the railway through the region north of Lake Superior was an incredible challenge. Even Van Horne referred to this as "two hundred miles [300 km] of engineering impossibility."

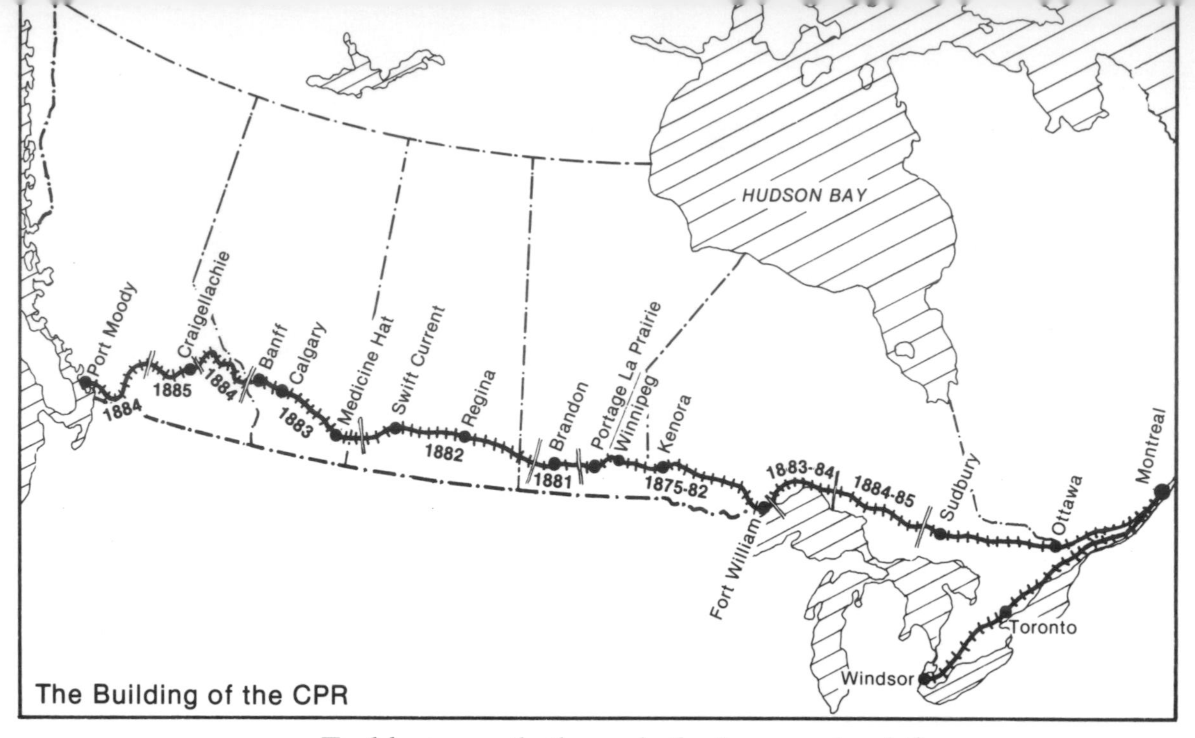

The Building of the CPR

To blast a path through the bare rock of the Canadian Shield, Van Horne had three factories making the new invention called dynamite. Explosions thundered all along the line. Some workers were blown up in accidents or injured by falling rock. When the blasting was finished, the workers had to push rock and rubble to fill in countless lakes and ponds. Mosquitoes and black flies buzzed around their heads. The dark forest seemed to stretch forever. To see what his men had to face, Van Horne once walked 130 kilometres along the Lake Superior route, and he learned why the job was going so slowly.

The worst parts were the muskegs. The men called muskeg swamps "bogs without bottom." Muskegs looked solid because they were covered with peat and grass, but they were full of water and they could swallow enormous amounts of rock and gravel without being filled. If they were not filled, they would swallow entire trains.

As the men fought the wilderness, Van Horne

no room for a railway on the canyon's edge, and the work was hard and slow. The men had to blast out every step of the route, as steamboats fought their way up the rapids to bring them supplies.

Among the workers in the Fraser Canyon were more than 6000 men who had come all the way from China to work on the railway. The Chinese labourers put up with racism as well as sickness, danger and loneliness, and they worked hard to push Onderdonk's line through the canyon. Many died in accidents and had to be buried along the way.

The Chinese labourers in British Columbia handled many of the most dangerous construction jobs, often for very low wages. They lived in squalid, separate construction camps.

Designing and constructing the trestle for this bridge over Stoney Creek on the eastern slopes of the Selkirk Mountains in British Columbia surely presented an awesome task.

As these crews were finishing the Fraser Canyon line, Van Horne's workers were advancing through the Kicking Horse Pass towards Rogers Pass. They had to build many long tunnels and hundreds of bridges and trestles. In some places they had to build roofs over the track to protect the trains from winter avalanches.

Finally, in the late fall of 1885, the two groups of workers drew close. There were only a few more spikes to drive, and then the Canadian Pacific Railway would be finished.

had to worry about another problem. The work was going slowly and costing too much. The CPR was running out of money. The company could not pay for equipment, and it could not even pay its men for the work they had done. Many workers had to spend the winter in the work camps, with bad food, poor shelter and no money. The workers were bitter. The government and the company owners were desperate.

Then rebellion broke out on the prairies. The Indian peoples were angry over the way the railway and the settlers had taken their land and killed the buffalo. Some of them wanted war, and in 1885 Louis Riel and his Métis people joined them. The Northwest Rebellion was on.

To stop the rebellion, Canada had to send soldiers to the prairies. Van Horne promised that the railway would get them there, even though the route across the rocks and bogs north of Lake Superior was not finished. Wherever there was track, railway cars carried the troops rapidly through the rugged northland. The soldiers were able to march across the gaps despite winter storms and terrible cold. At every work camp, Van Horne's crews had food and coffee ready for them.

The troops reached Winnipeg in just a week. Soon they were in Saskatchewan, where they defeated Riel. The Northwest Rebellion came quickly to an end.

Most Canadians believed that by carrying the troops to the Northwest so quickly, the CPR had proved its value to the nation. Now the government was willing to provide more money to help the company. Van Horne was able to pay his workers and buy the supplies they needed. Soon the tracks were being laid again.

Into the Mountains

In 1885 trains could run all the way from Halifax, Nova Scotia, to Calgary in Alberta. Towns were sprouting all along the railway. Settlers were riding the CPR toward new homes on the prairies. Van Horne knew that when the settlers began to grow wheat, his railway would make a lot of money carrying it to market, so he shipped seeds to the prairies and told his men to build grain elevators to store wheat.

The last part of the Pacific railway still had to be built, and it would be the toughest part of all. Even when Van Horne's workers were moving rapidly across the prairies, no one knew what route they would follow through the mountains and canyons of British Columbia.

Year after year, explorers and surveyors struggled across the valleys and snowy peaks, risking their lives as they searched for passes through the mountain ranges. Sometimes they got lost and ran out of food, and often trails that had looked perfect led into dead ends. Finally, in 1882, after years of searching, Major A.B. Rogers solved the last piece of the British Columbia puzzle. He found a pass in the wild Selkirk Mountains, and it was named after him. The railway could go through.

By now the railway builders were working from both ends. Van Horne's men who had crossed the prairies plunged into the Rocky Mountains. Other workers led by a contractor named Andrew Onderdonk had started from the Pacific coast and were working slowly toward them.

Onderdonk's men had been labouring for years in the deep canyon where the Fraser River cuts through the mountains of British Columbia's Coast Range to find its way to the Pacific. There seemed

NOTICE!

YALE, B. C., SEPT. 26, 1885.

AS OUR LAST RAIL FROM THE PACIFIC HAS BEEN LAID IN Eagle Pass to-day,

And the balance of work undertaken by the CANADIAN PACIFIC RAILWAY COMPANY between Savona and point of junction in Eagle Pass will be Completed for the Season on WEDNESDAY,

ALL EMPLOYEES WILL BE DISCHARGED

On the Evening of September Thirtieth.

Application for position in the Operation Department for the present may be made to M. J. HANEY, but the above portion of line will not be operated until Notice is given to that effect by the VICE PRESIDENT.

ALL ACCOUNTS

Should be liquidated before the TENTH PROXIMO, at Yale, as the books of the Company should be closed on that day.

A. Onderdonk.

The Last Spike

In November 1885 Canada waited for a great moment. The two teams of workers had met in Eagle Pass. Van Horne had decided to name the meeting place with a Scottish word—"Craigellachie." That meant strength and determination to two of the CPR's founders, George Stephen and Donald Smith. There, the last spike would be driven, and the great railway would be complete.

Would there be thousands of people, and a golden spike covered with diamonds? Van Horne said no. It was hard to predict exactly when the job would be finished, and in any case the CPR could barely afford any ceremony. "The last spike will be just as good an iron one as there is between Montreal and Vancouver," said Van Horne, "and anyone who wants to see it driven will have to pay full fare."

The driving of the last spike at Craigellachie, British Columbia symbolized the completion of the railway, but in fact much still had to be done before it could be in full operation.

Van Horne was being as tough as ever, but there was still quite a crowd at Craigellachie on the morning of November 7, 1885. Major Rogers put a spike in place. Donald Smith raised the hammer. He swung, but his aim was off, and he bent the spike. Quickly they put in another spike and Smith hammered it down. The railway was complete. There was a silence, and then everyone began to cheer.

William Van Horne had to say something. What could he say? Perhaps he thought of all the "impossible" jobs he had promised to do, or about all the problems they had faced. Maybe he thought of the workers who had done so much and the men lying buried along the railway track. But he did not say any of that. He simply said, "All I can say is that the work has been done well in every way."

Then they walked back to the train, and the conductor of Canada's first transcontinental train cried out, "All aboard for the Pacific!"

Sir John A. Macdonald

The building of the Pacific railway was a great national effort, though it was a private company, the CPR, that built and ran the line. As Canada's first prime minister, Sir John A. Macdonald promised a transcontinental railway in order to spread Confederation from sea to sea.

Prime Minister Macdonald always supported the railway, but it brought him a great many troubles. The first plan to build the railway collapsed in 1873 when Macdonald had to resign in disgrace for accepting money from the company that got the railway contract. Macdonald became prime minister again five years later, however, and his support was very important to the railway. People complained that it was either taking too long or costing too much. When Macdonald listened to them, Van Horne and the CPR feared that he might abandon them.

In July 1886, as Sir John and Lady Agnes Macdonald rode the CPR on their first visit to the West, the prime minister told a story. Once his friends had told him that building the CPR would take so long that he would only see it from heaven. His enemies claimed he would see it from hell. Thanks to the speed with which Van Horne and his workers had finished the job, Sir John A. could happily announce, "I am now taking a horizontal view."

Lady Agnes loved the view so much that she rode part of the way through the mountains on the "buffer bar" at the front of the locomotive.

I travelled on the Buffer beam from Laggan to Pt. Moody. Every step of the way. Mr. Egan made me a lovely seat with a box and cushions, right in front of the Engine, and down the Kicking Horse Pass, he and I and Mr. F. White flew on the big Engine in delightful style. I was not at all afraid. I don't know how I am going to ride in a car, like a Christian, any more, after the delights of a cushioned cowcatcher!

Even among those wonderful loops near Rogers Pass, or on the steep grade of the Kicking Horse, or on the sharp curves of the magnificent Fraser Canyon, so steady was the Engine that I felt perfectly secure and the only damage we did from Ottawa to the sea, was to kill a lovely little fat Pig, whom an error of judgment led under the engine near Nicomen, yesterday morning.

Letter from Lady Macdonald
to William Van Horne

Founders of the CPR

George Stephen

Donald Smith

George Stephen and Donald Smith were cousins. They were both born in Scotland, and they came separately to Canada. Donald Smith became a Hudson's Bay Company fur trader in Labrador and then in Manitoba. George Stephen became the president of the Bank of Montreal.

In 1877 Smith persuaded his cousin that they should invest their money in a railway from Minnesota, in the United States, to Winnipeg, Manitoba. The railway succeeded. The two men became very rich, and they caught the railway bug.

Three years later, the cousins became partners in the Canadian Pacific Railway Company. Even though Donald Smith and Prime Minister Macdonald disliked each other, the company won the contract to build Canada's railway to the Pacific.

Stephen and Smith drove a hard bargain. They would find the money to build and run the railway, but in exchange Canada gave their company huge amounts of land and a promise that no other railway would be allowed to compete with theirs for twenty years.

While the railway was being built, the cousins sometimes thought it would swallow up all their money and all they had borrowed. If the CPR could not finish its task, they would be ruined, for they had gambled every penny on the railway.

It was Stephen and Smith who hired Van Horne to build the CPR and gave him the greatest challenge of his life. Van Horne's success saved the company, and all three became richer and more powerful than ever.

The Man in the Private Car

Building the Canadian Pacific Railway had made William Van Horne a Canadian. He never went back to the United States. Instead he built a big house in Montreal, where he and his wife Lucy and their children had been living since 1883. He had been "general boss of everything and everybody" while the CPR was being built. Now that it was finished, he became president of the company and continued to run the line he had built.

There were still plenty of challenges. Because the CPR crossed from one side of North America to the other, it carried goods from all over the world. Silks from China soon rode on the CPR on their way to Europe. In a few years, Van Horne had CPR ships sailing both the Atlantic and the Pacific oceans. He wanted more people to settle on the CPR's lands, so his railway carried newcomers to the West as well as wheat to the East. He wanted tourists to see the beauty of Canada, so he had hotels built all along the line, and he even suggested how they should look. Soon the CPR meant hotels, ships, telegraphs, mines and many things beside the railway.

Not everyone was pleased. Farmers complained that the railway charged too much for hauling wheat. Settlers said that the CPR owned too much land and ran too many businesses. No one could compete, they said, for the CPR could ruin them just by moving their station away. There were no other railway companies on the prairies, because the government had promised the CPR that it would have no competition there for many years. In the West, the CPR had so much power that people

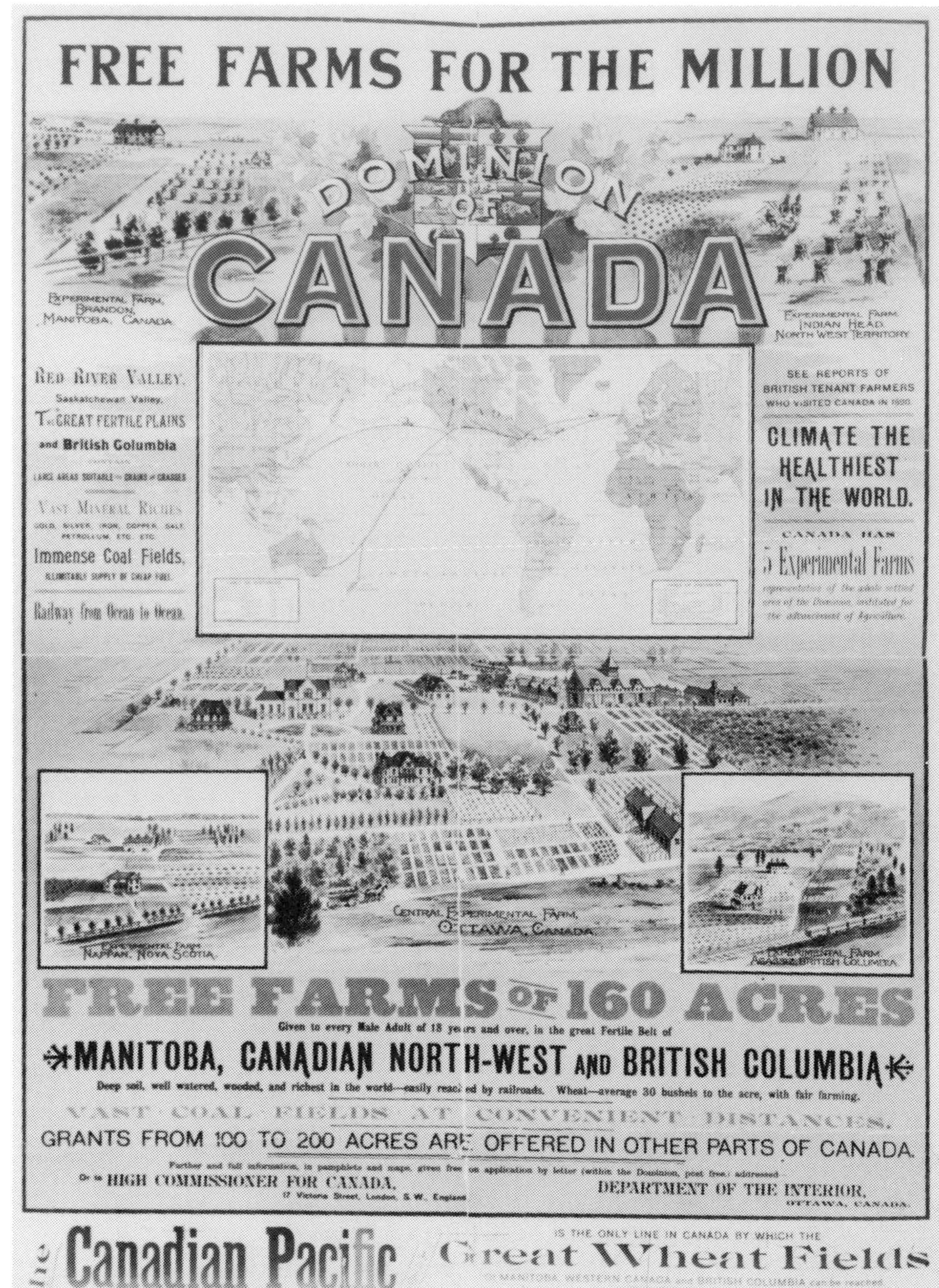
FREE FARMS FOR THE MILLION
DOMINION OF
CANADA
Experimental Farm, Brandon, Manitoba, Canada
Experimental Farm Indian Head North West Territory
Red River Valley,
Saskatchewan Valley,
The Great Fertile Plains
and British Columbia
Vast Mineral Riches
Immense Coal Fields.
Railway from Ocean to Ocean.
SEE REPORTS OF
BRITISH TENANT FARMERS
CLIMATE THE HEALTHIEST IN THE WORLD.
CANADA HAS
5 Experimental Farms
Central Experimental Farm, Ottawa, Canada
Experimental Farm Nappan, Nova Scotia
FREE FARMS OF 160 ACRES
Given to every Male Adult of 18 years and over, in the great Fertile Belt of
MANITOBA, CANADIAN NORTH-WEST AND BRITISH COLUMBIA
Deep soil, well watered, wooded, and richest in the world—easily reached by railroads. Wheat—average 30 bushels to the acre, with fair farming.
VAST COAL FIELDS AT CONVENIENT DISTANCES.
GRANTS FROM 100 TO 200 ACRES ARE OFFERED IN OTHER PARTS OF CANADA.
HIGH COMMISSIONER FOR CANADA,
17 Victoria Street, London, S.W., England
DEPARTMENT OF THE INTERIOR,
OTTAWA, CANADA.
The Canadian Pacific RAILWAY
IS THE ONLY LINE IN CANADA BY WHICH THE
Great Wheat Fields

blamed it for everything that went wrong.

Van Horne paid little attention. He wanted the CPR to be as big and successful as he could make it, and he bargained hard for every money-making opportunity. For years he kept an eye on everything along the railway, from telegraph poles to advertisements. He even told the railway cooks what to serve in the dining cars.

Accommodations in day and sleeping cars could be very luxurious. Many passengers, however, travelled in cars which were far less fancy but still provided reasonable accommodation for travel across Canada.

Van Horne called his summer residence Covenhoven, which was the name of his grandmother's family.

The Van Hornes built a summer home on Minister's Island near St. Andrews, New Brunswick, and started a cattle ranch in Manitoba. Van Horne became a Canadian citizen and even accepted a knighthood. He collected paintings and became a good painter himself. He travelled a lot. He went to Europe to collect art. He visited old friends in the United States. He helped build a railway in Cuba. His curiosity remained as great as ever. He once said there was so much to do that he wanted to live to be five hundred years old.

William Van Horne loved big things, "big and bulgy like myself," he said. Even the beds in the CPR sleeping cars were bigger than usual, because he wanted them that way. The CPR had given him what he wanted most: a railway to build and run. He was grateful. "I have more regard for the CPR than for anything in the world, aside from my wife and children," he said.

Young William Van Horne had dreamed of riding in his own railway car. The CPR let him keep one all his life. It was called "Saskatchewan," and whenever he grew restless he climbed aboard and travelled off along the railway he had helped to build, stopping where he liked to see the changes and talk to the men. When he died in 1915, every train in the CPR stopped running for five minutes in memory of William Cornelius Van Horne, the railway general. Then "Saskatchewan" carried him away to be buried.

Sir William Van Horne's funeral train.

A Tribute
to William Van Horne

"Canadians even today, have no realization of the work he did or of what they owe him . . . the fertility of his genius and resource were boundless, as were the skill and force with which he brought his conceptions to reality. Alongside these mighty powers lay . . . playgrounds in which he took his recreation and amusement—such as painting, the collection of works of art, porcelain, etc., and his sleight-of-hand and trickplaying. In fact, there was nothing that he saw which did not interest him and to which he did not apply himself to some extent.

To all this was added a noble simplicity of character, inexhaustible good humour, great kindliness and an almost boyish enthusiasm and love of tricks and pranks . . . .

The great central zone of Sir William was his insatiable appetite for work [and] the vigour and enthusiasm with which he could throw himself into it . . ."

George Tate Blackstock, K.C., Toronto 1916

Railway Towns: Winnipeg

Winnipeg was a small village before the railways arrived but when railway building started, the town became the "Gateway to the West" as well as the capital of Manitoba. A railway south to the United States was started in 1877, and soon after that Winnipeg became the centre of construction for the CPR's line across the prairies.

When Van Horne arrived in 1881, Winnipeg was the liveliest boom town in North America. It was growing so fast that anyone who owned land there could become rich overnight.

Railways and Winnipeg continued to grow together. Millions of immigrants rode the CPR to settle in the West. They all passed through Winnipeg, and so did the crops and livestock that they shipped east. Some of the immigrants settled in Winnipeg, which was the largest city on the prairies, and the CPR employed some of them to work in its yards and repair works.

Railway Towns: Regina

Until 1882 most settlers in Saskatchewan lived and travelled along the Saskatchewan River, and the capital of the territory was at Battleford, a fort on the river. The CPR, however, decided to build its line far south of the river. To be on the railway line, the capital moved south to a treeless plain beside Pile o' Bones Creek. There were only three people living there.

Pile o' Bones was renamed Regina (which means "queen" in Latin). A couple of months later, the first train arrived with William Van Horne aboard. The city was on the map, and ever since it has been one of the most important cities on the prairies.

The place had been called Pile o' Bones because of all the buffalo skeletons piled there. The CPR even made money out of those. Van Horne had them loaded on trains and hauled east for fertilizer.

Railway Towns: Banff

"I never in all my explorations saw such a matchless scene," said a young surveyor named Tom Wilson when an Indian guide showed him Lake Louise in the summer of 1882. Since then, many other people have said the same thing, and the beautiful lake among the glaciers has become one of Canada's favourite places to visit.

Van Horne knew that the magnificent scenery of the Rocky Mountains could become part of the CPR's business. When prospectors found hot springs bubbling out of the ground a few kilometres from Lake Louise, a nearby mountain station called Siding 29 became the resort town of Banff. The hot springs became Canada's first national park in 1885, and a few years later the CPR built the huge Banff Hot Springs Hotel. Travellers and tourists have been heading for Banff ever since.

Railway Towns: Vancouver

The city of Vancouver did not exist when the CPR decided that the western terminal of the railway would be on the wooded harbour called Burrard Inlet on British Columbia's Pacific coast.

In 1884 Van Horne went to inspect the B.C. part of the railway. He chose the site where the line would end, and he even had a name for the place, which he expected would grow into a great city. It would be called Vancouver, after the sea captain who had explored Burrard Inlet nearly a century earlier.

In 1885 the townsite of Vancouver was marked out in the forest. The railway reached it the next year, and Vancouver quickly grew into the great city that Van Horne had imagined.

For Discovery

1. The Grand Trunk, Great Western and Intercolonial railways were all smaller railways which had been built before the CPR. Choose one of these railways and write two or three paragraphs about its development. On a map of Canada, trace its route.

2. You are the head of a crew at "End of Track" north of Lake Superior. Mr. Van Horne has asked you to describe a typical day. Include details about both living conditions and working conditions.

3. Imagine you are an immigrant settler riding the CPR from Montreal to your new home in western Canada. Describe your journey and your new home in a letter to your family. Include information about the route you took, the landscape around your new home and your new neighbours.

4. Imagine that you have been chosen to interview William Van Horne on November 7, 1885, at the driving of the last spike. With a classmate, make up a set of questions and answers that might have taken place during such an interview.

5. A well-known Canadian historian has written: "A legend was born that the CPR saved Canada in 1885. Indeed, it was Louis Riel who saved the CPR." Explain what was going wrong for the railway in 1885 and how Riel could be said to have saved it.

6. Create a travel brochure, including pictures, for a tour across Canada by train today. As you plan your brochure, think about these questions.

   - Which towns and cities will you visit?
   - What places of interest will you visit in these places?
   - How much will the tour cost and how long will it be?
   - What kinds of accommodation will be offered?

7. The railway meant many changes for the Indians and Métis whose lands it crossed. Find out about the way of life of these people before the railway came and about the changes and adjustments they needed to make after it came.

8. Canadian Pacific is the largest and wealthiest private company in Canada today. While it is still involved with railways, it has many other business interests as well. Find out what some of these interests are.

Index